As I walk

by
ANNA ADIDEPVORAPHAN

As I walk

Copyright © 2020 by Anna Adidepvoraphan.

Paperback ISBN: 978-1-952982-48-4
Ebook ISBN: 978-1-952982-49-1

All rights reserved. No part in this book may be produced and transmitted in any form or by any means, electronic, or mechanical, including photocopying, recording, or by any information storage and retrieval system, without permission in writing from the copyright owner.

The views expressed in this work are solely those of the author and do not necessarily reflect the views of the publisher hereby disclaims any responsibility for them.

Published by Green Sage Agency   11/03/2020

Green Sage Agency
1-888-366-9989
inquiry@greensageagency.com

foreword

This work that Anna has made is an important step in relationship to the development of our consciousness and unconscious modality. What I mean by this is that each person who looks at Anna's work will see a reflection of an aspect within themselves. The creativity that is within each piece of work is unique.

To be asked to write this foreword is a great privilege and I wish to acknowledge Anna and the gift that she has in producing this work not only for herself but for the larger community. Anna has dropped the mask and is ready to step into the world as the creative artist and by doing so she is in her own way helping to awaken others to their own power of creativity, be that in a conscious awareness or even tapping into the unconsciousness to become aware.

It is with this hope that I offer this introduction to Anna's magnificent work. I hope that those who are touched by Anna's work will tell others and pass this inspiration on.

Colette Garside
Founder: Winds of Change
Colour Academy
Stratford upon Avon
Warwickshire
UK

Preface

When you read the words
And gaze upon the drawings
Thoughts may appear in your mind
Whatever it maybe
Let it settle slowly
Then change whatever "you" into "I"
And let it linger a little while
For that may well be
The start of a beautiful journey

Anna Adidepvoraphan

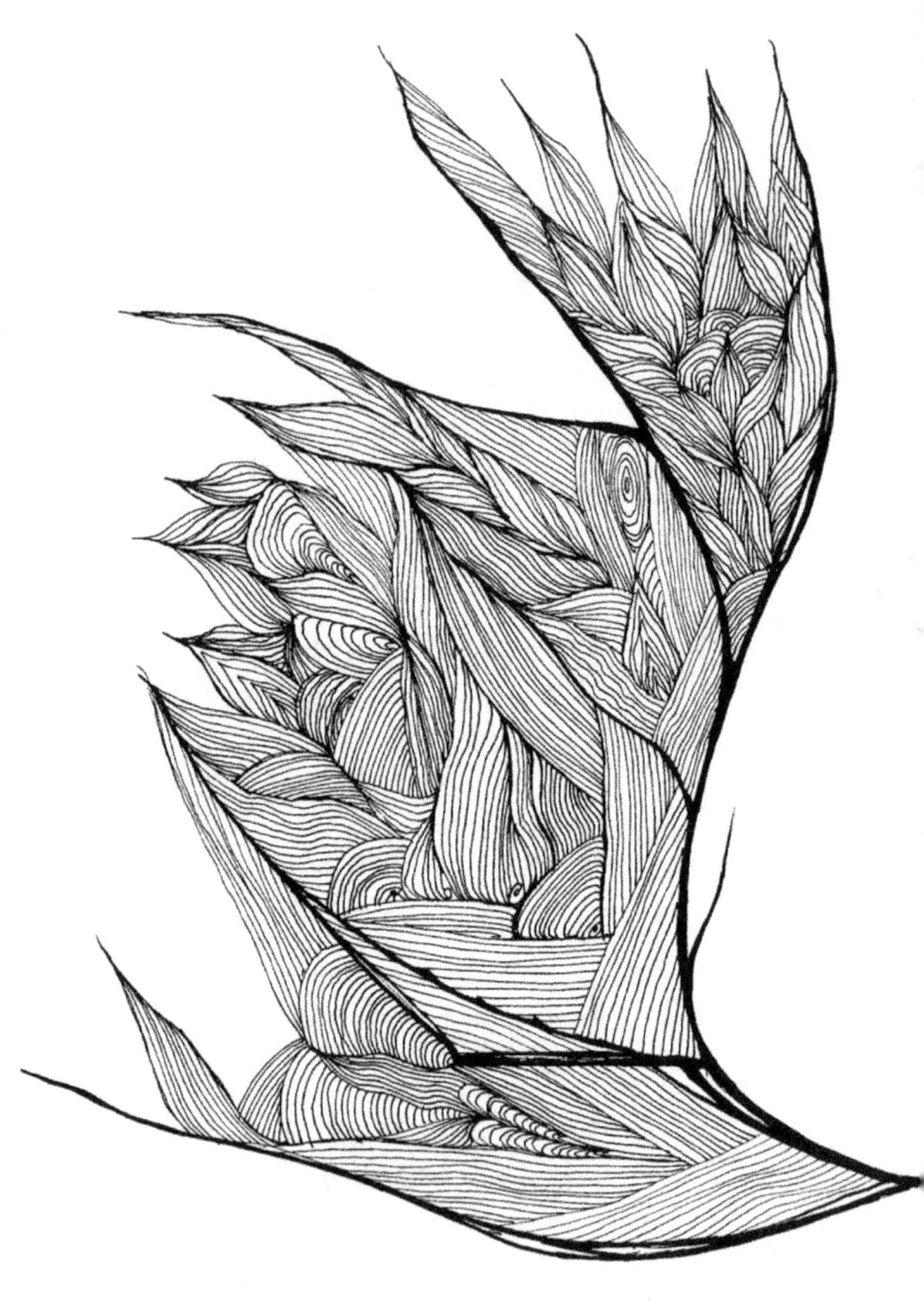

I am as I was created to be
I am free
Nothing whatsoever can influence me
Unless I allow
I need do nothing

*As above
So below*

Everything is as it should be
There is no rush
There is no fear
In its own time
Everything shall be clear

*Arrogant nor humble
Weak nor invincible*

It just is

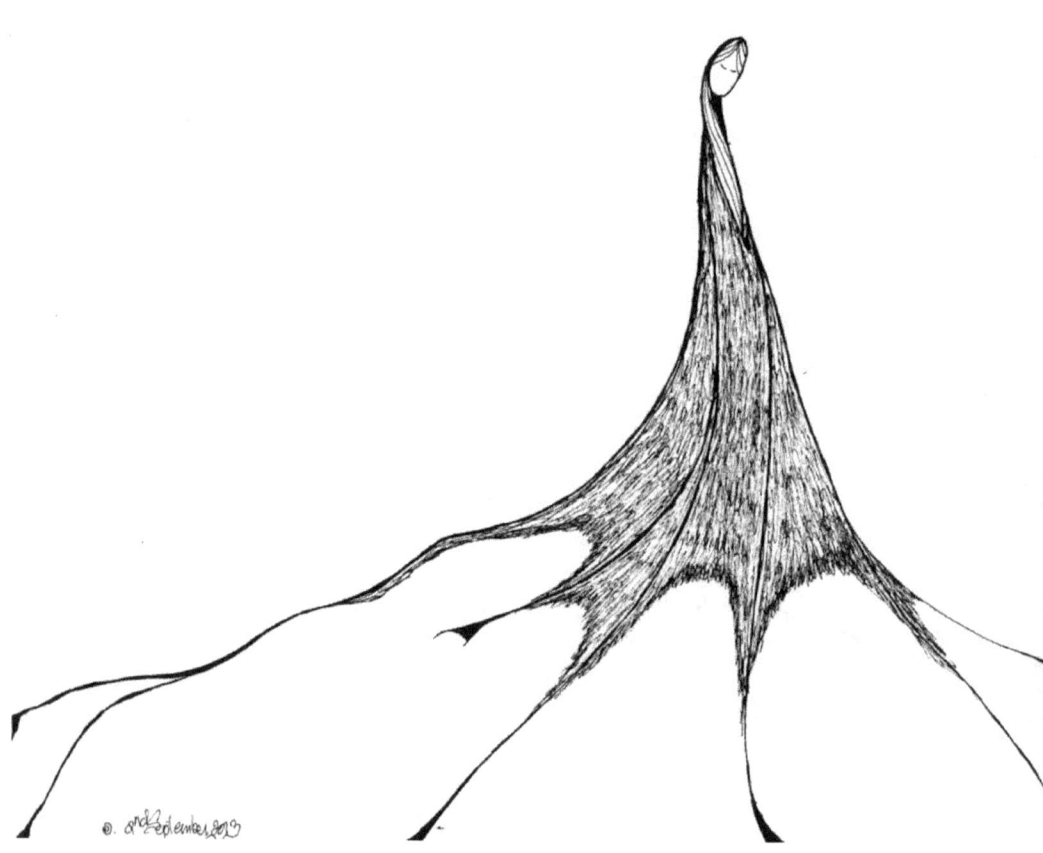

Slowly my grasp is loosening
My tears start flowing
I get down on my knees
My face in my hands
I am sorry
I can't suffer for you
Though I've tried
I can't bear your burden
No matter how I tried
Please forgive me
For I still love you

Oh how she weeps
Her tears run deep
My guilt she bears
Until I come to care

I use my scale
I judge to no avail
I feed my ego
With pride and anger
Sorry now I say
Please forgive me, I pray

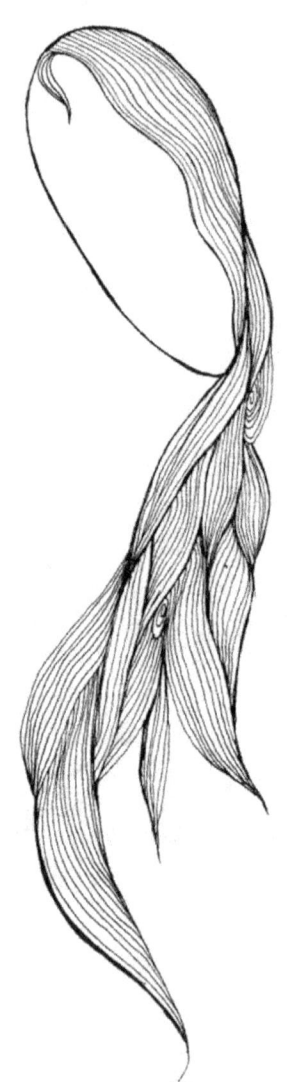

I can simplify my life
I cannot simplify yours
I can de-construct my wall
I cannot de-construct yours
… so it is

I respect me
So I respect you
I love me
So I love you

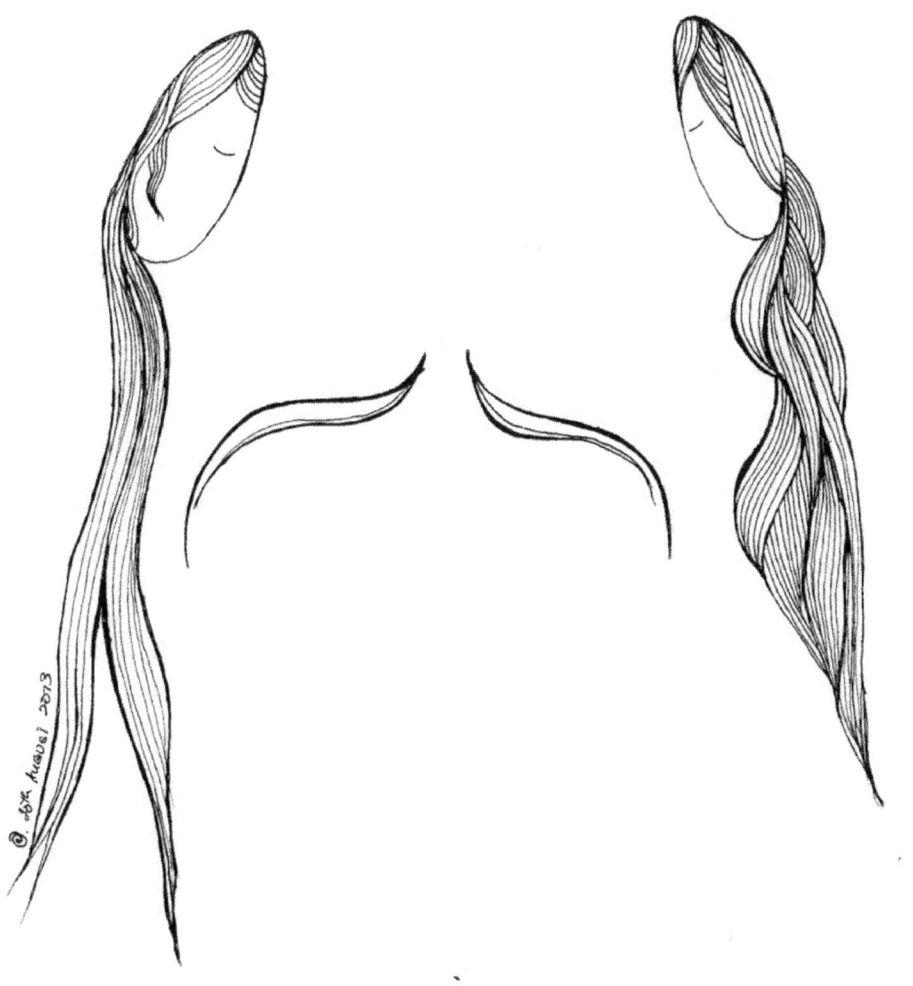

A violent storm
A gentle breeze
A willow stands
Through all
With ease

Layer by layer
I shed my skin
So shine
The light within

With a smile comes a tear
With joy comes sorrow
I embrace it all
And live without fear

This cloak of 'self'
I wear no more
Feeling exposed
Sheltered with love
For this being that is me

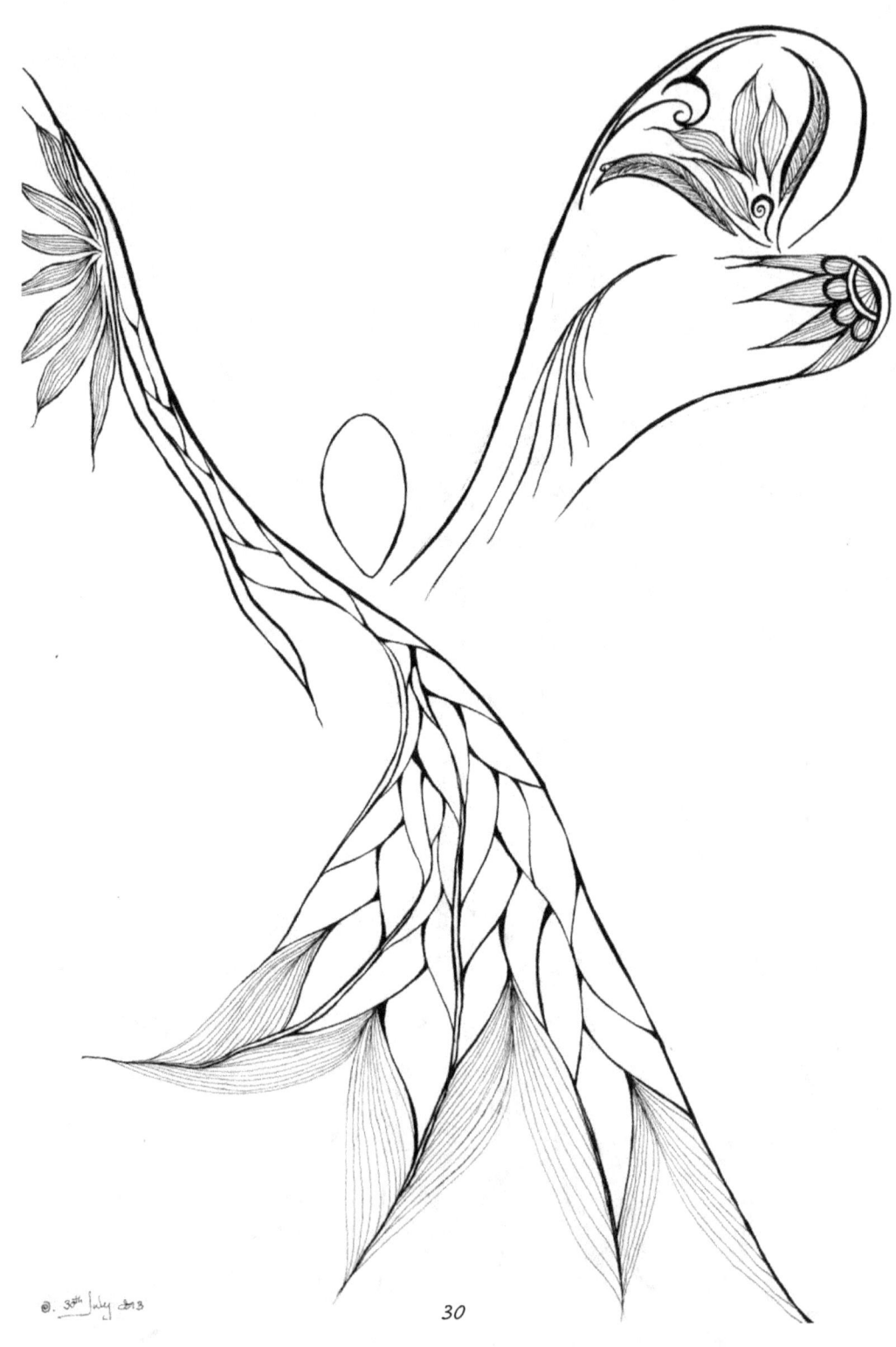

I rejoice
The song of life
I mourn
The deepest sorrow

I am alive

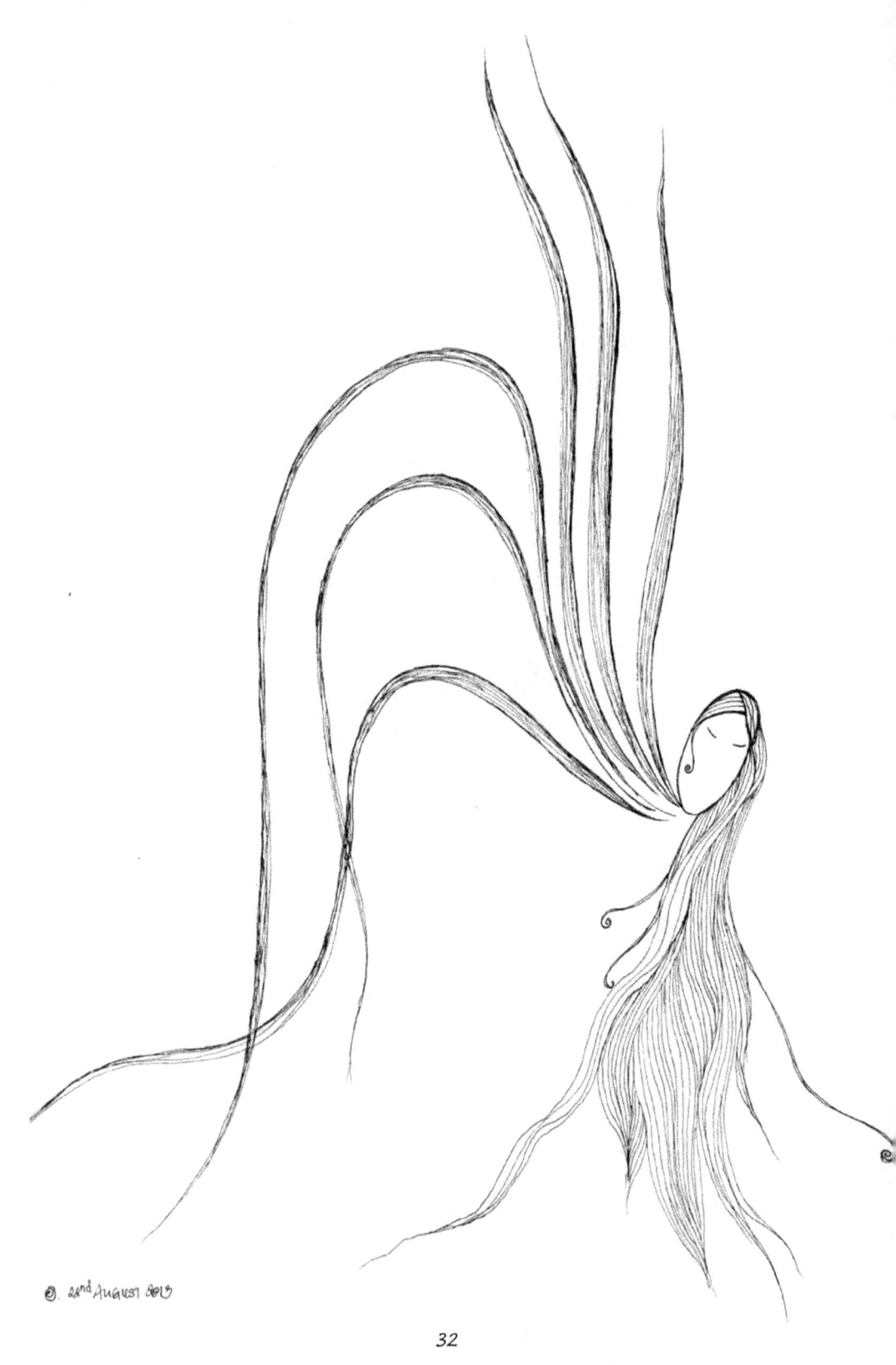

I give
I receive
No debt
No expectation

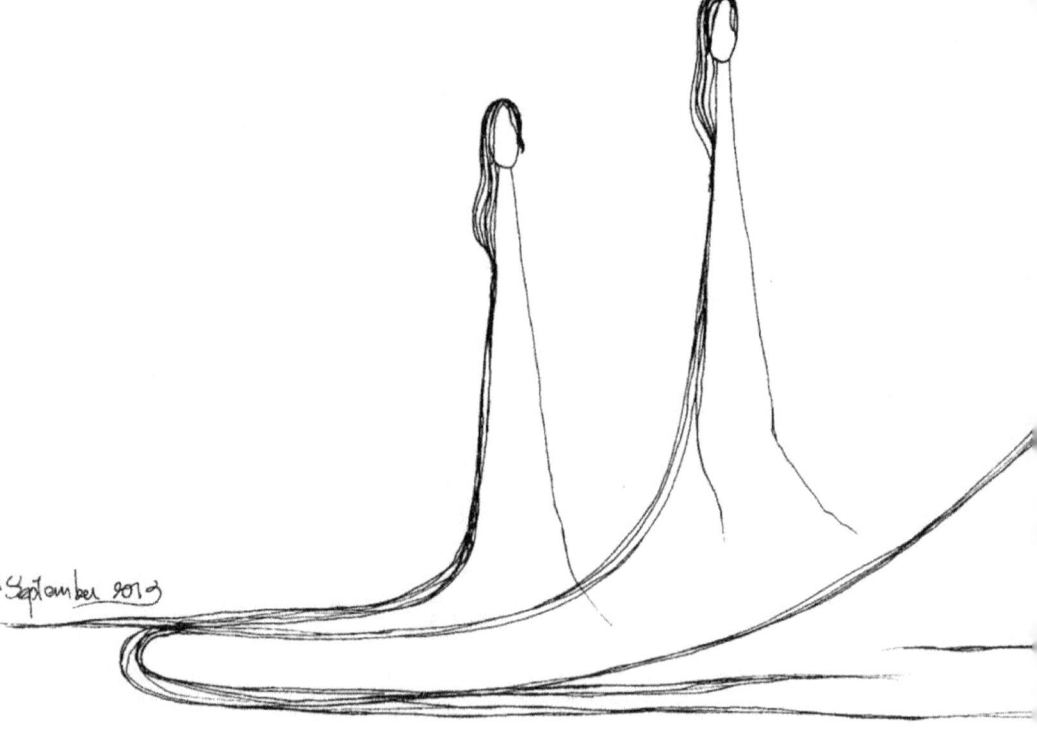

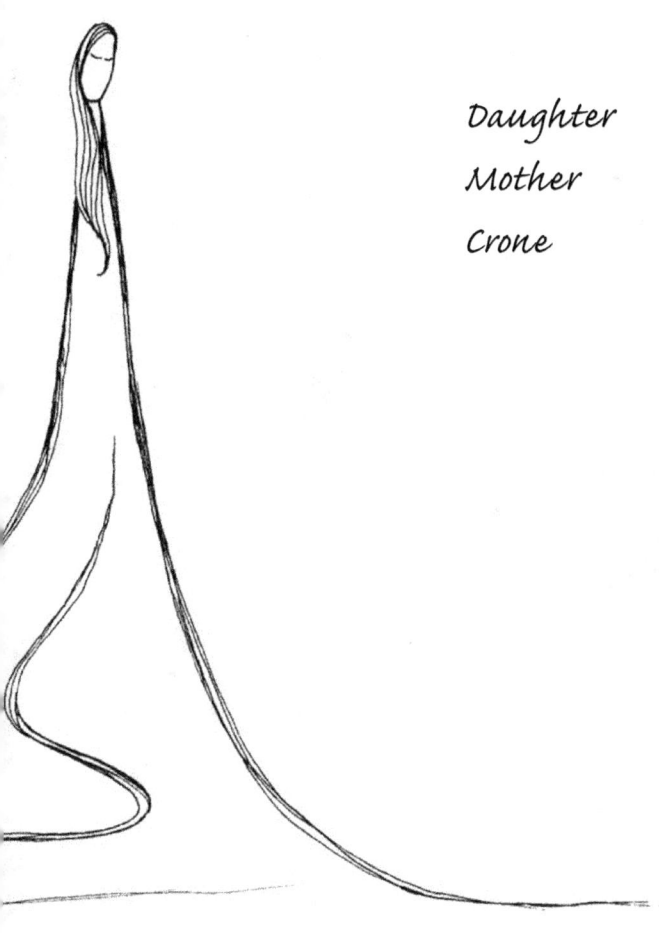

Daughter
Mother
Crone

I see beauty in you
I am beautiful too

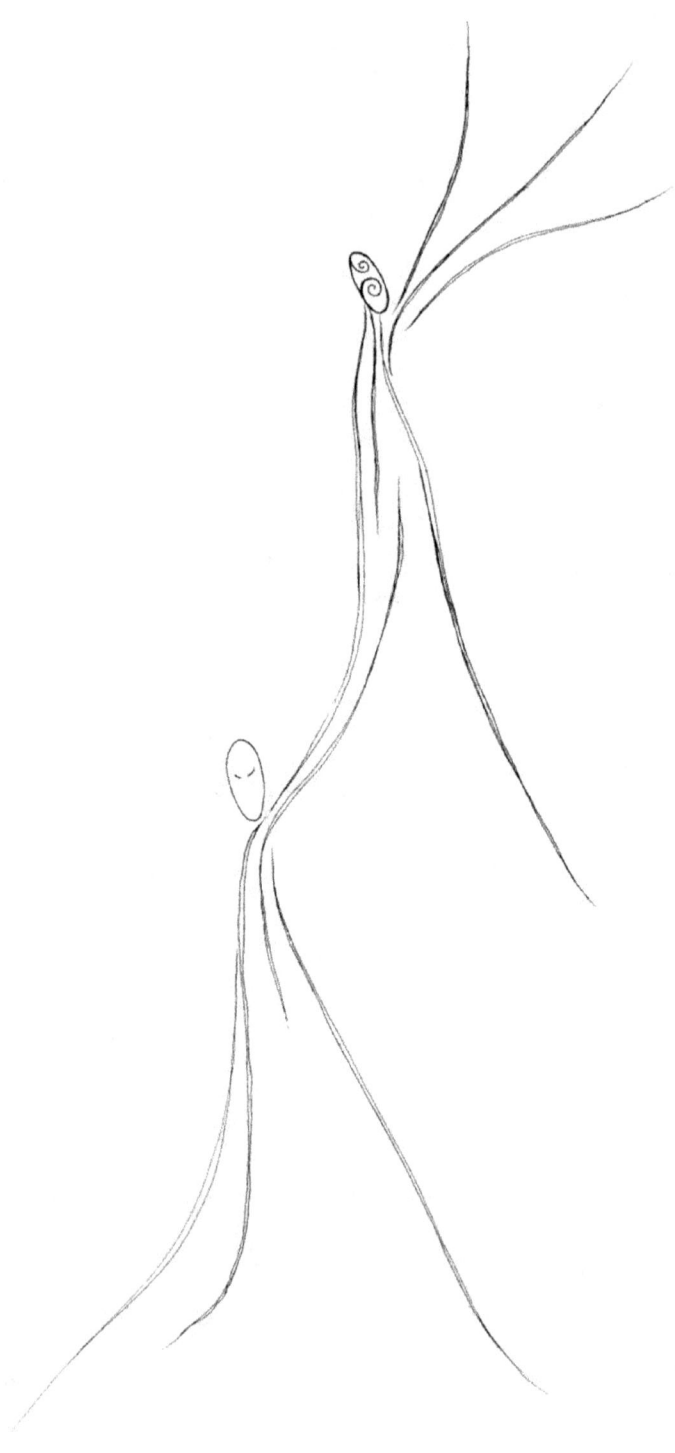

Take me by the hand
Lead me to the promised land

Perfections
Imperfections
Expectations
Frustrations
For naught is the struggle

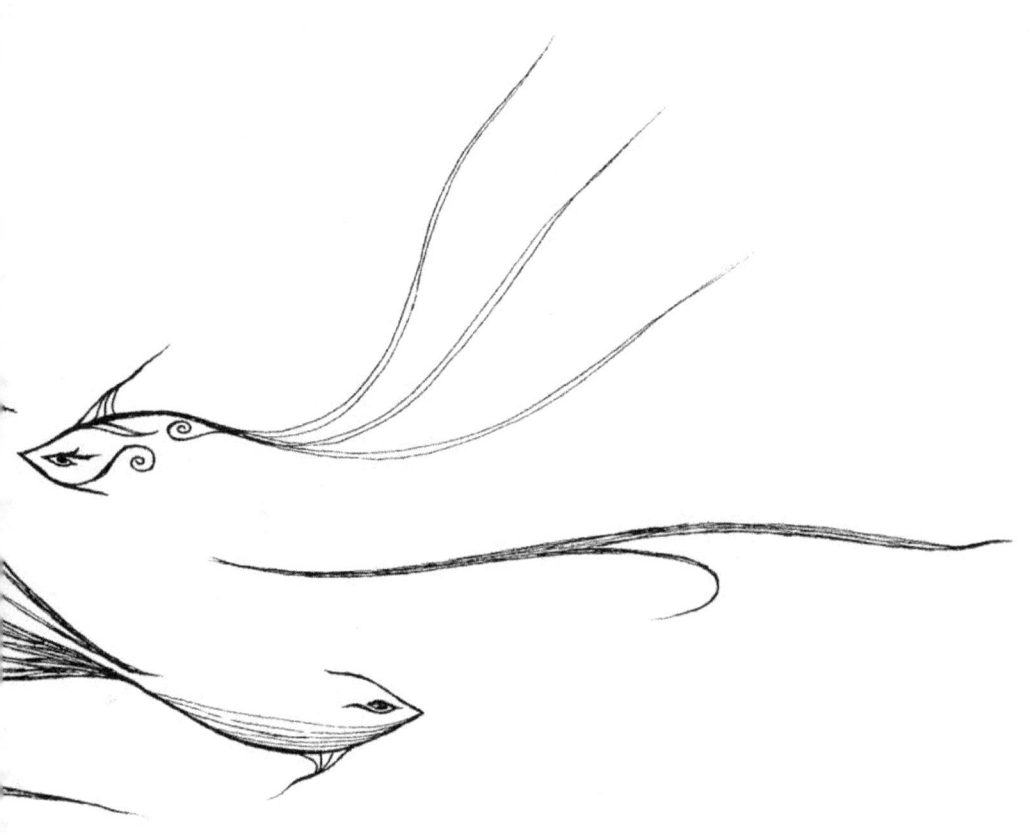

No one can hurt me
... but me

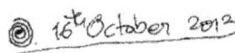

I burn down in flame
To rise up again
With glory to my name

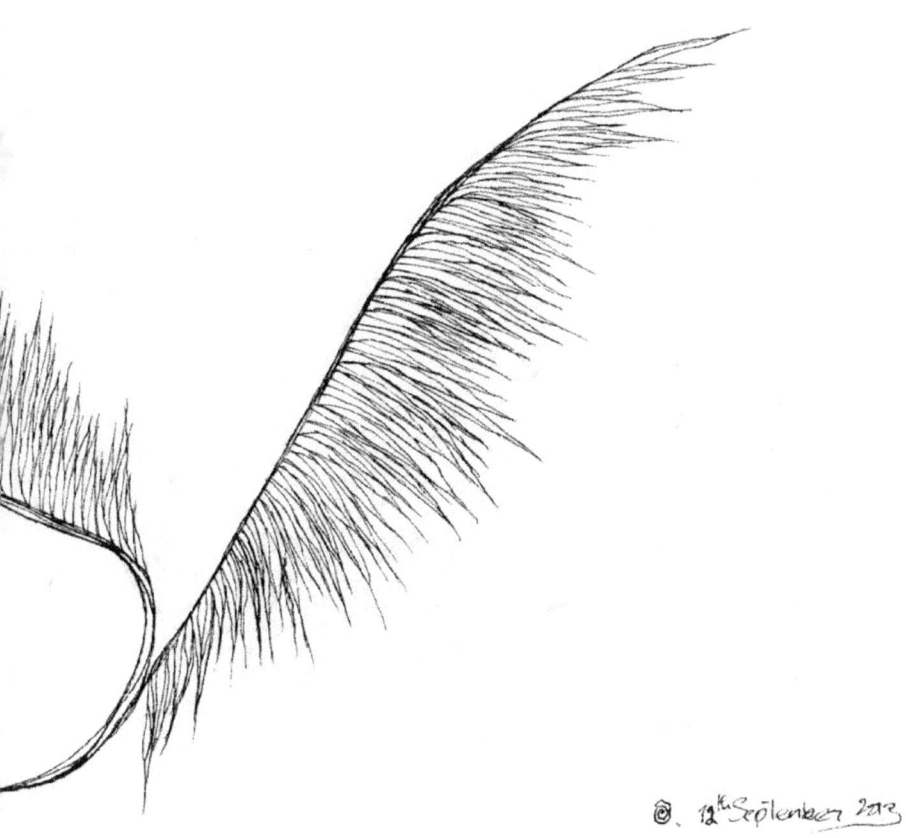

I stand within the walls of the prison
Built from my own expectations
I look in the mirror ...
The face of my worst enemy

© 12th September 2013

A single seed
I need nurture
In love
And in wonder

The past is like a shadow
It is just there
I try to grab at it
But to what gain

©. 13th September 2013

Pebble after pebble I put in my pocket
Pebbles of expectations
Pebbles of regrets
I let them drop, one by one
Now I hold not a single one

Inner wanting
Leads to outward struggling
Accept the wanting
It becomes nothing

© 2nd September 2023

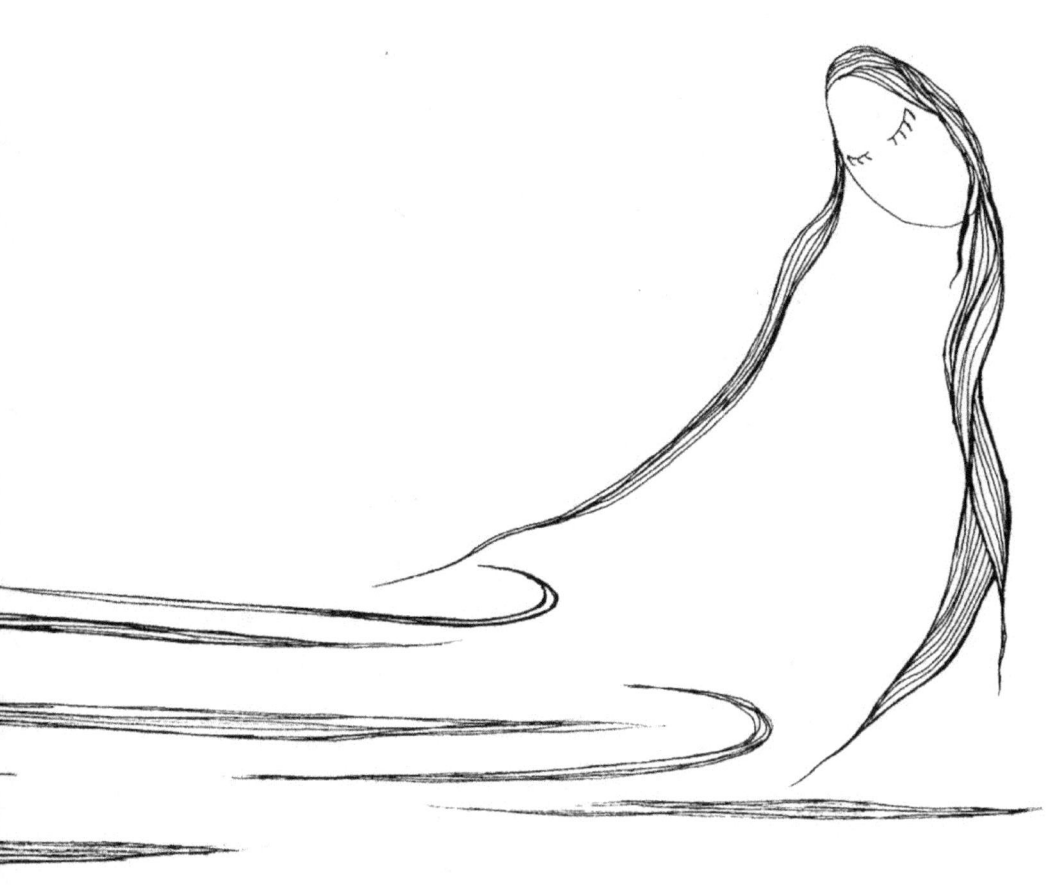

I look into your eyes
My heart echoes
With the fear inside
I follow the thread
And bring it to light

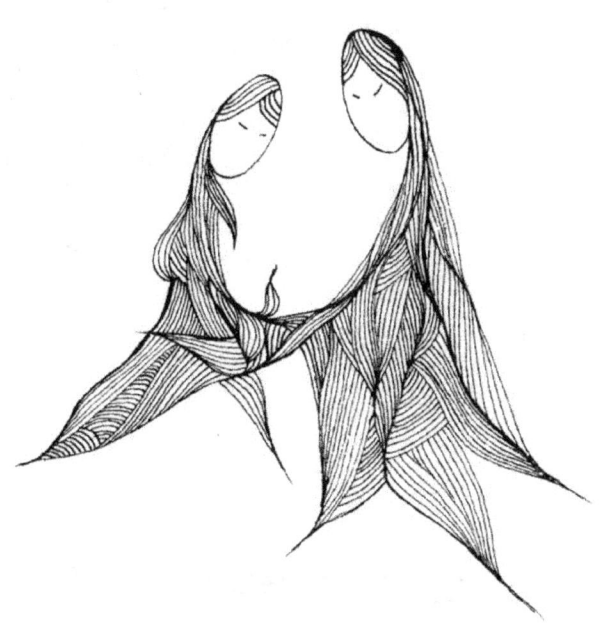

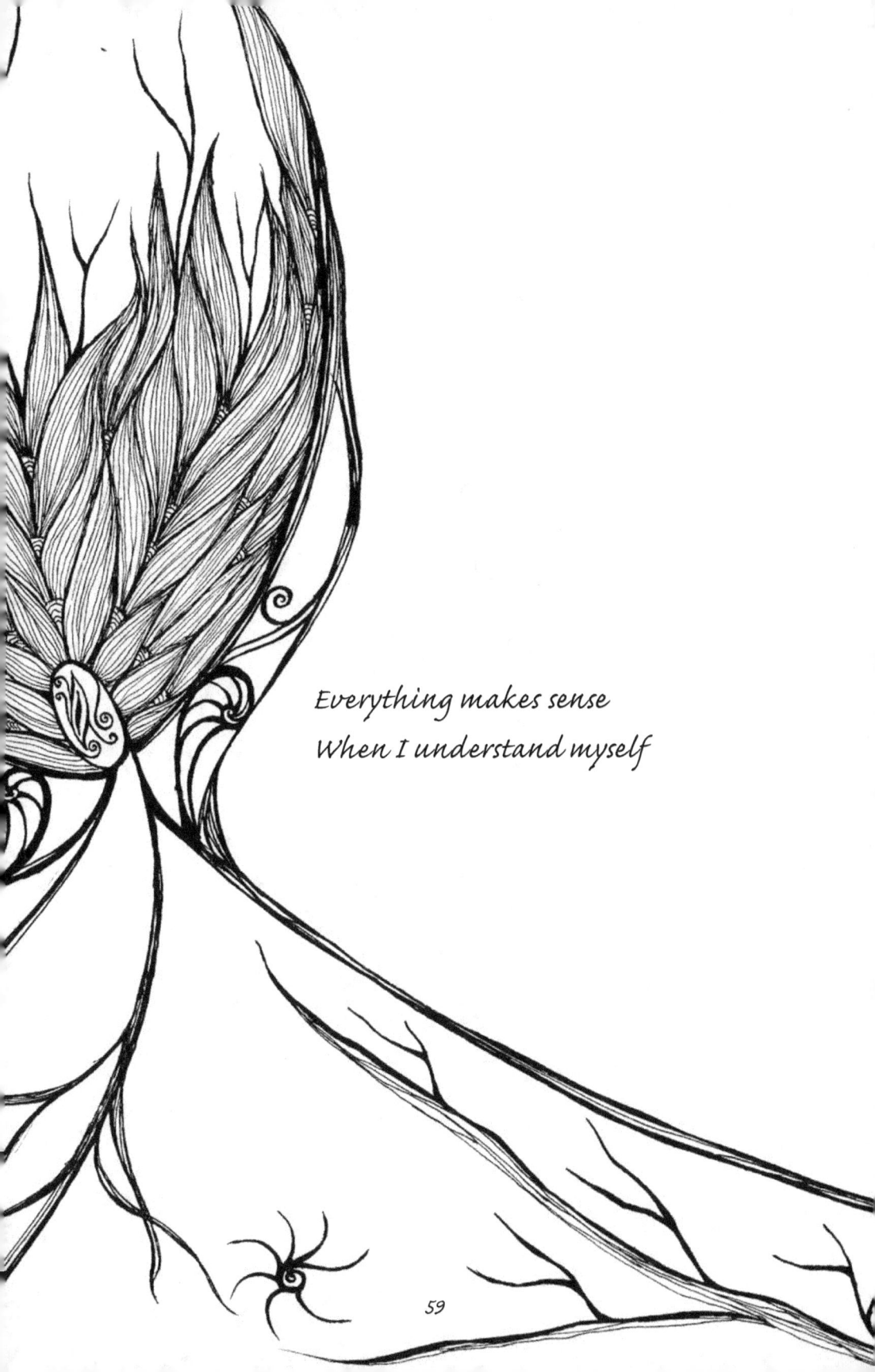

Everything makes sense
When I understand myself

The sun shines on me
As it does on everyone
The rain falls on me
As it does on everyone
I am a being
As is everyone

Open your heart
Feel the love
There lies abundance

In my heart lies the wisdom
I look inward and touch the jewel in the lotus

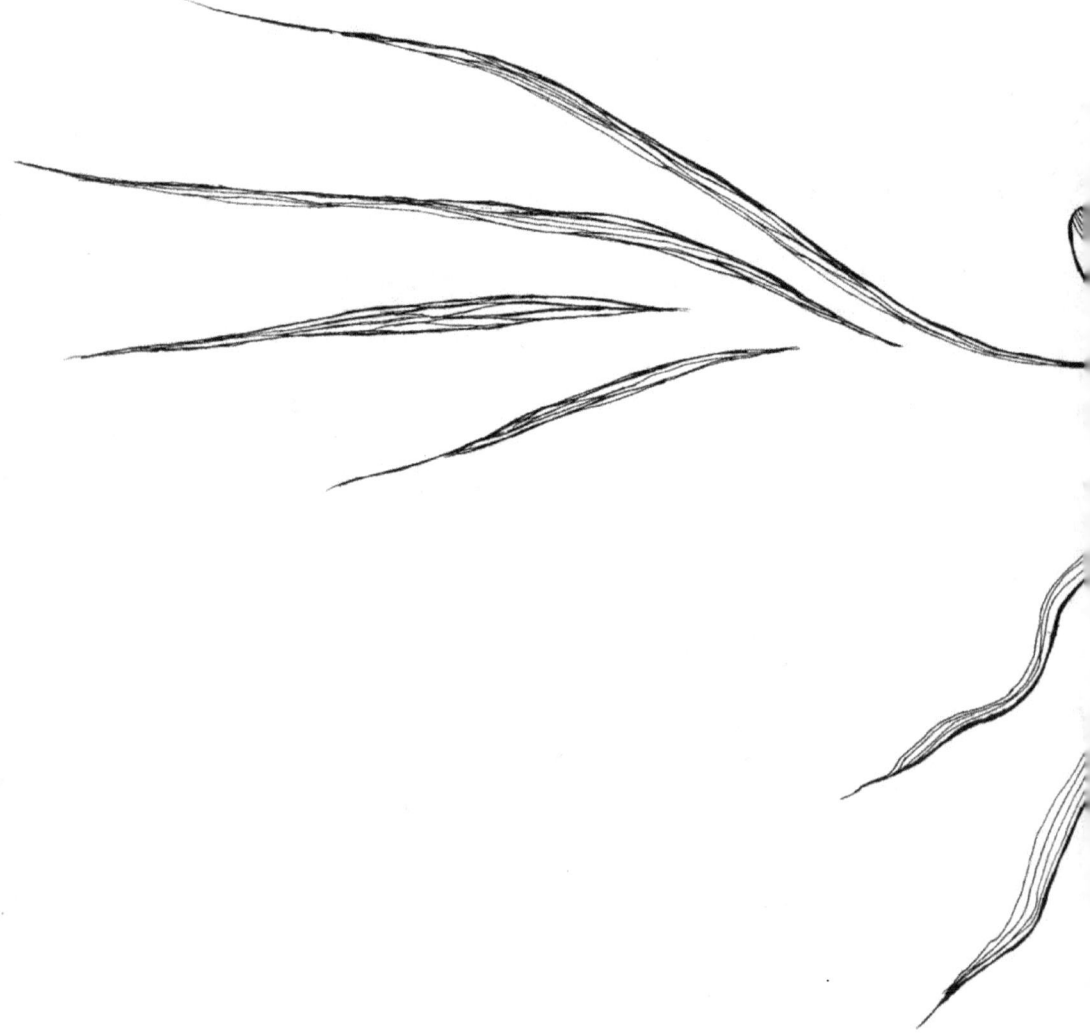

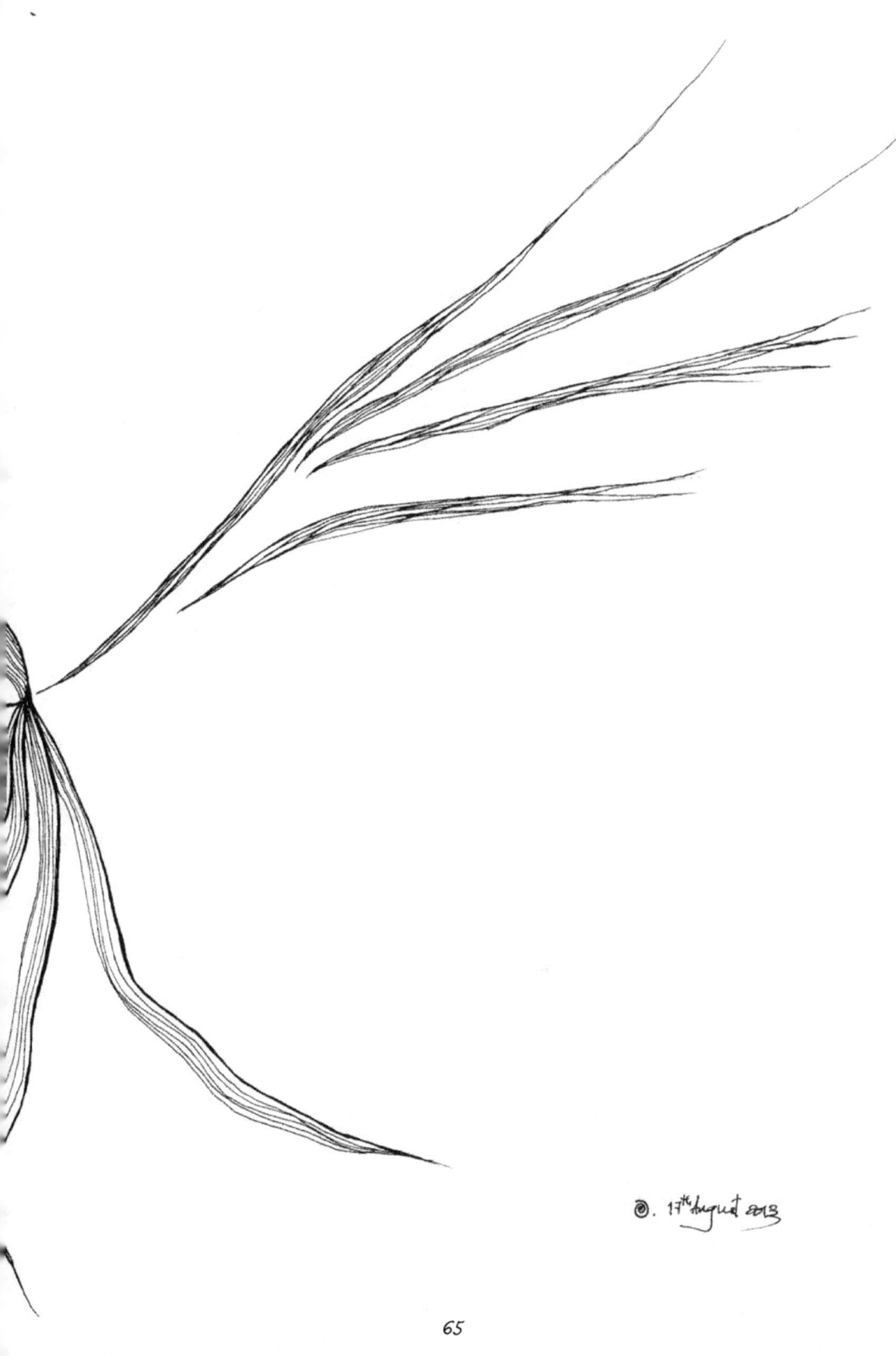

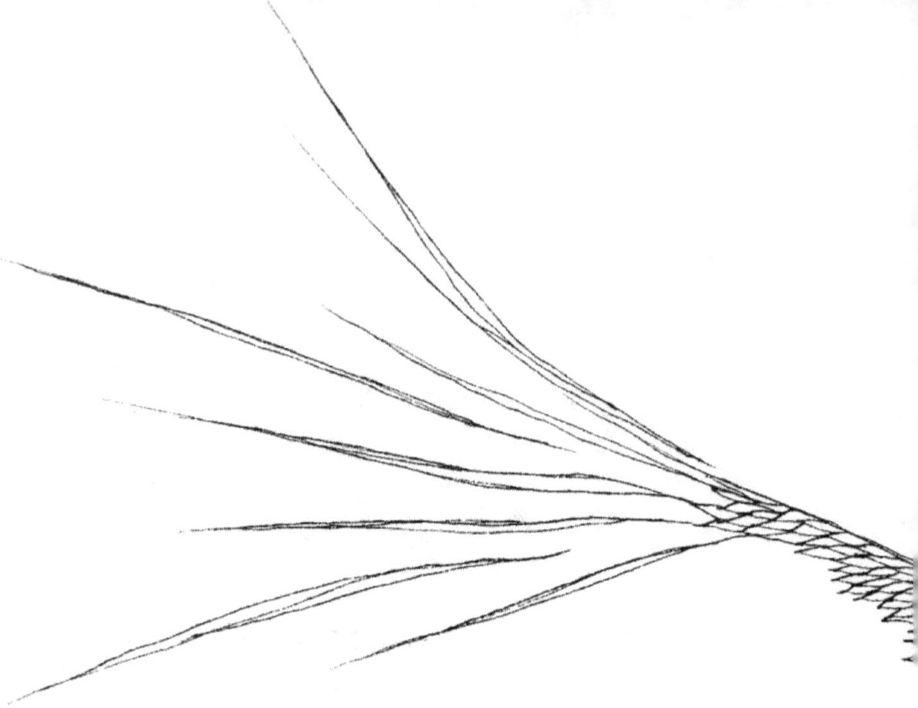

I can take to the sky
And fly on high
There is no limit to what I can do
So can you

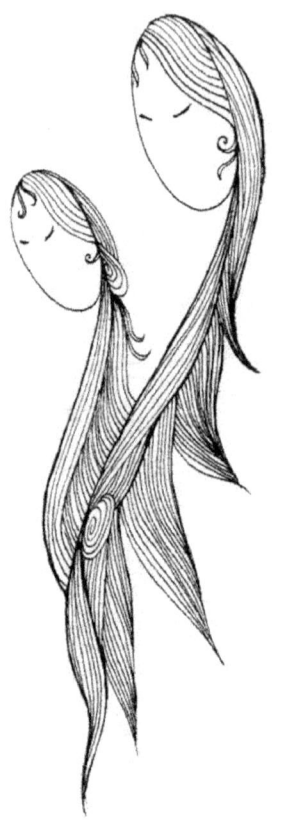

I love you naught for what you do
I love you naught for what you don't do
I just love you

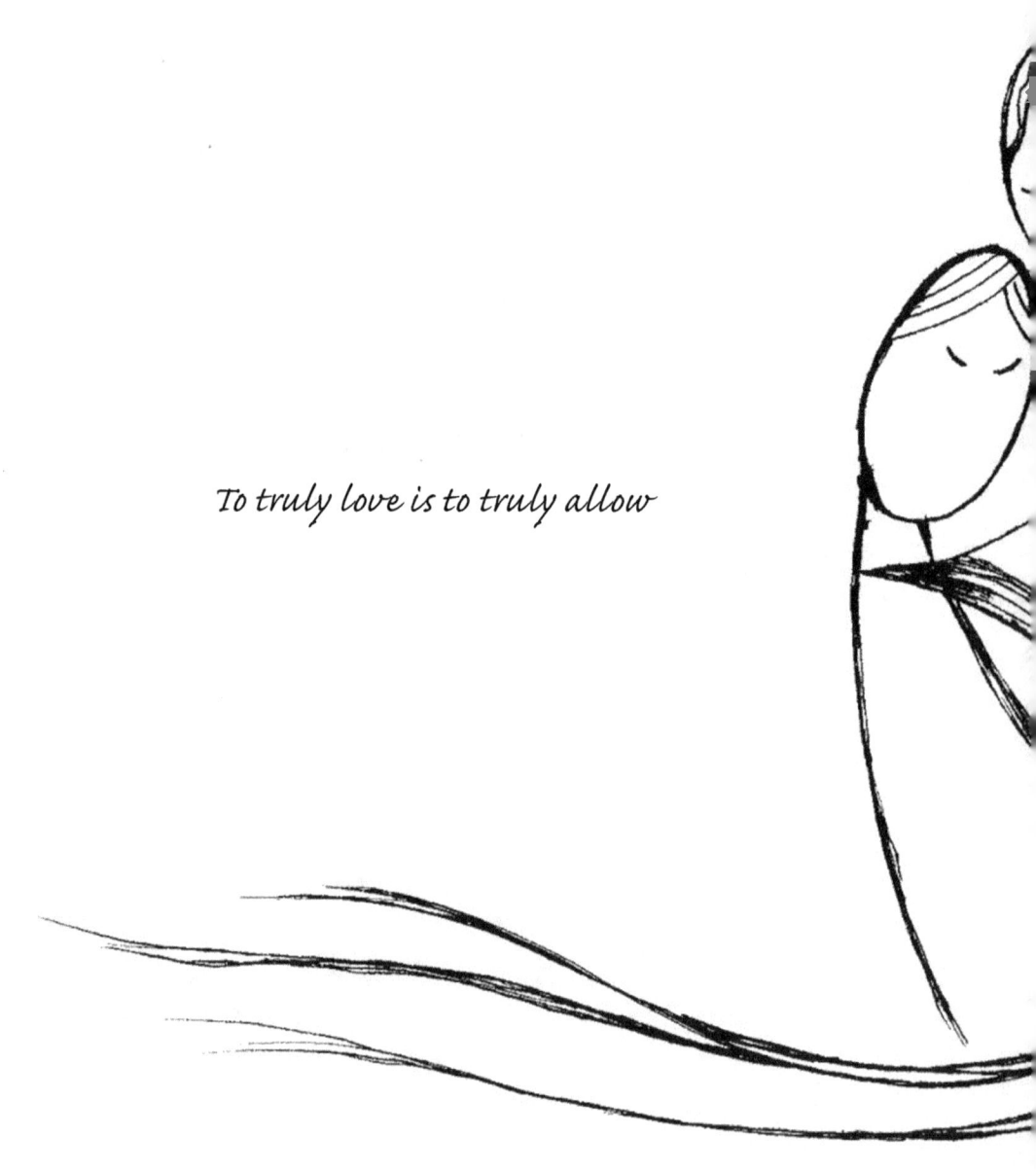

To truly love is to truly allow

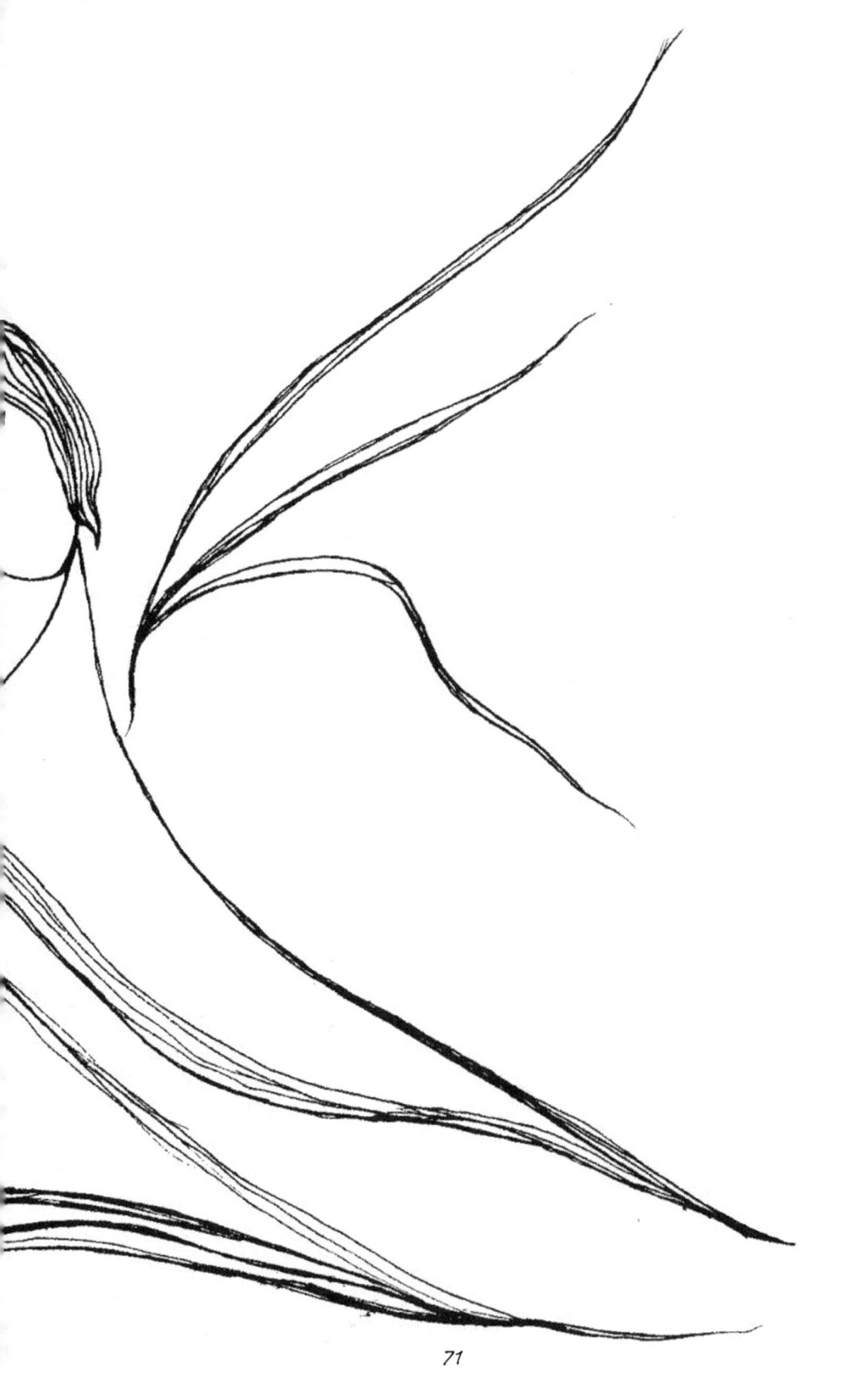

*Oh how my heart sings
With the joy of giving
When I rejoice
The joy of receiving*

With thread of love
I weave my coat
Of brilliant colours
And all kind of love

As above
I rise up to the glory
So below
I reach down to all the misery

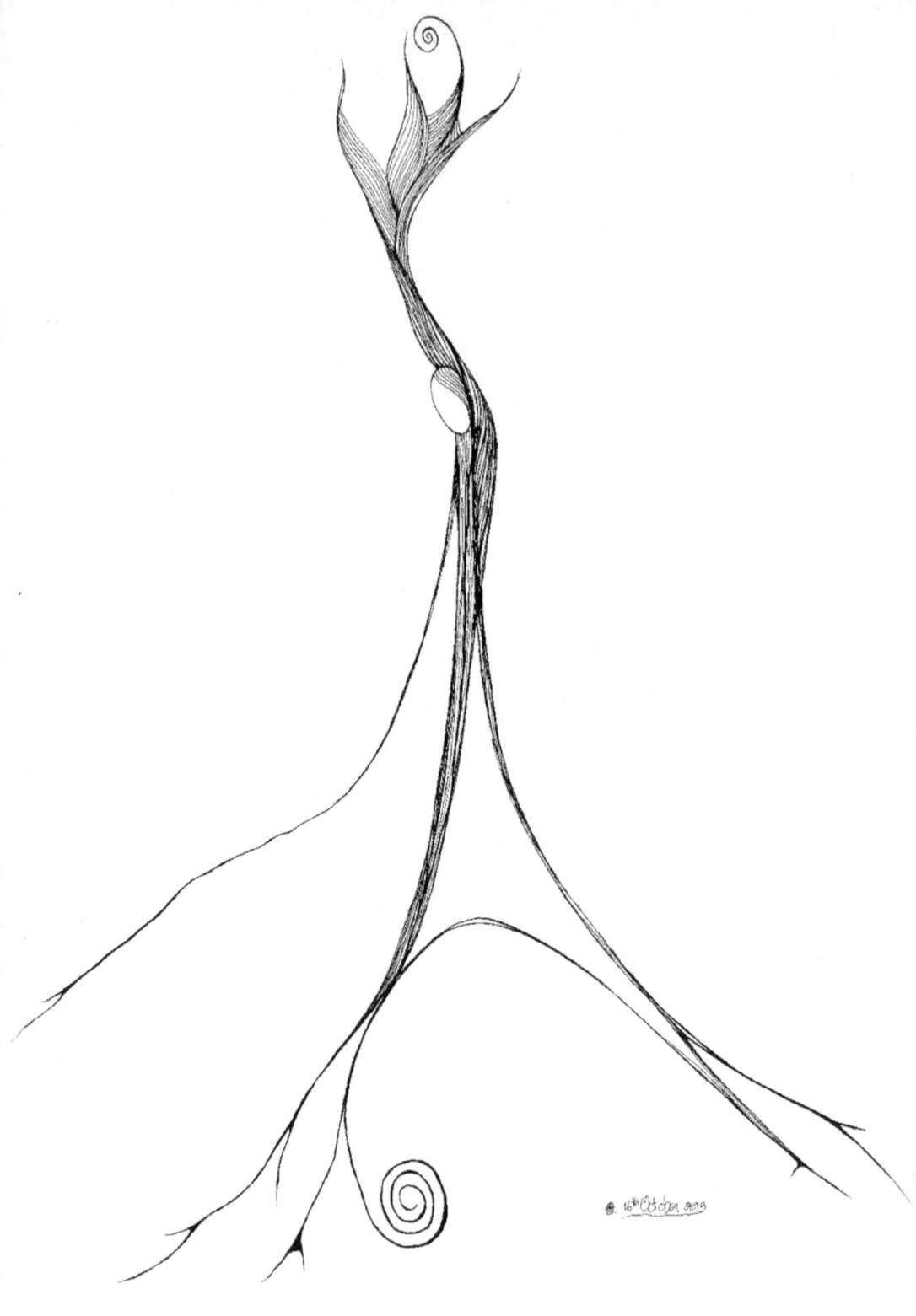

I wake up feeling scared and small
I take a deep breath
I embrace it all
I stand tall

A lost voice
No longer
'tis my choice
Even if I blunder

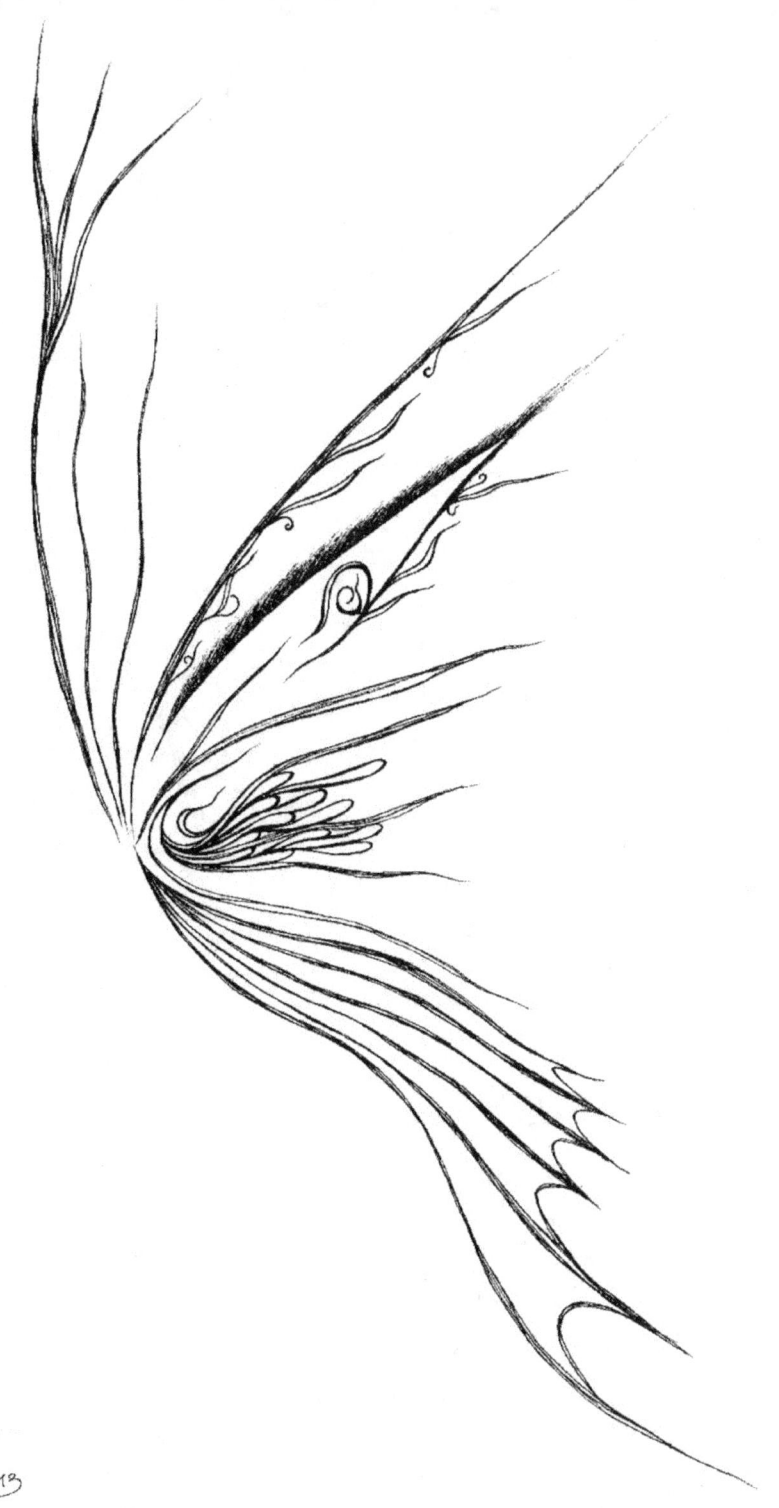

Like a child, I take the first step
Like a child, I stumble and I fall
Like a child, I get up again and again

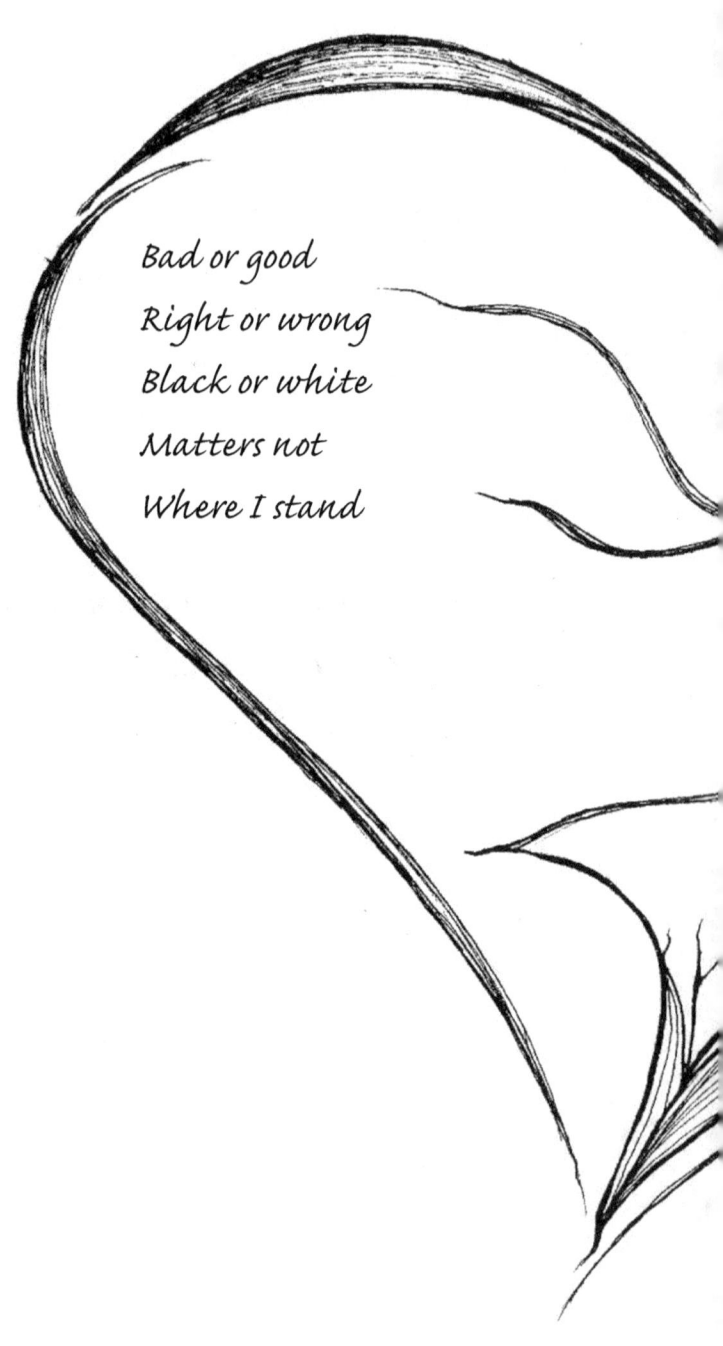

Bad or good
Right or wrong
Black or white
Matters not
Where I stand

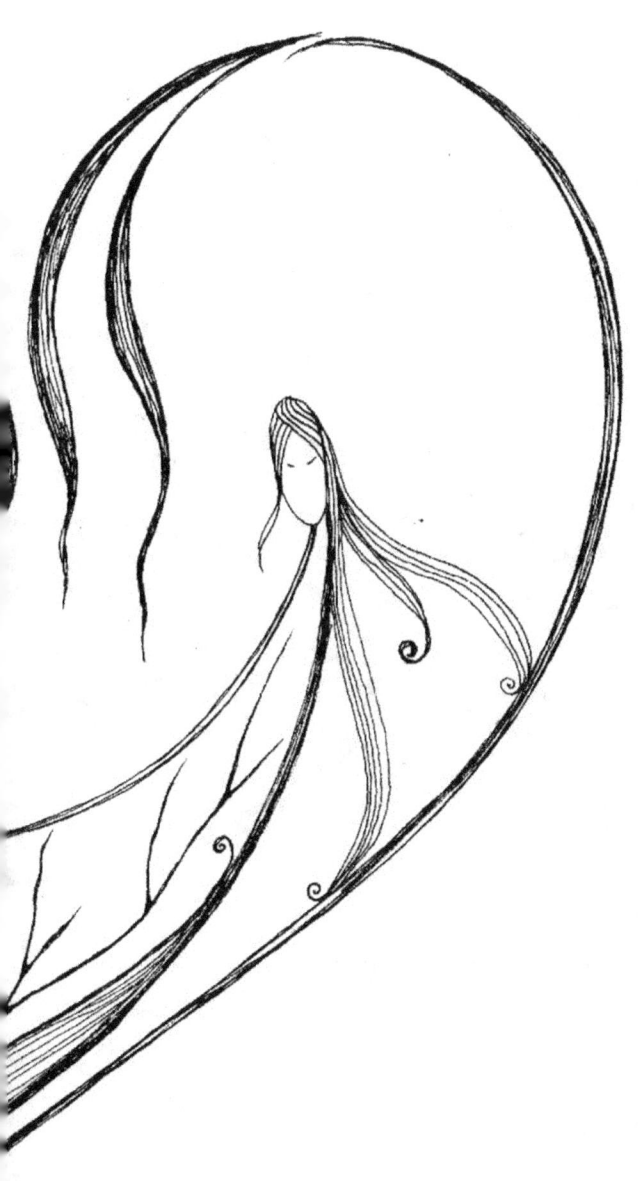

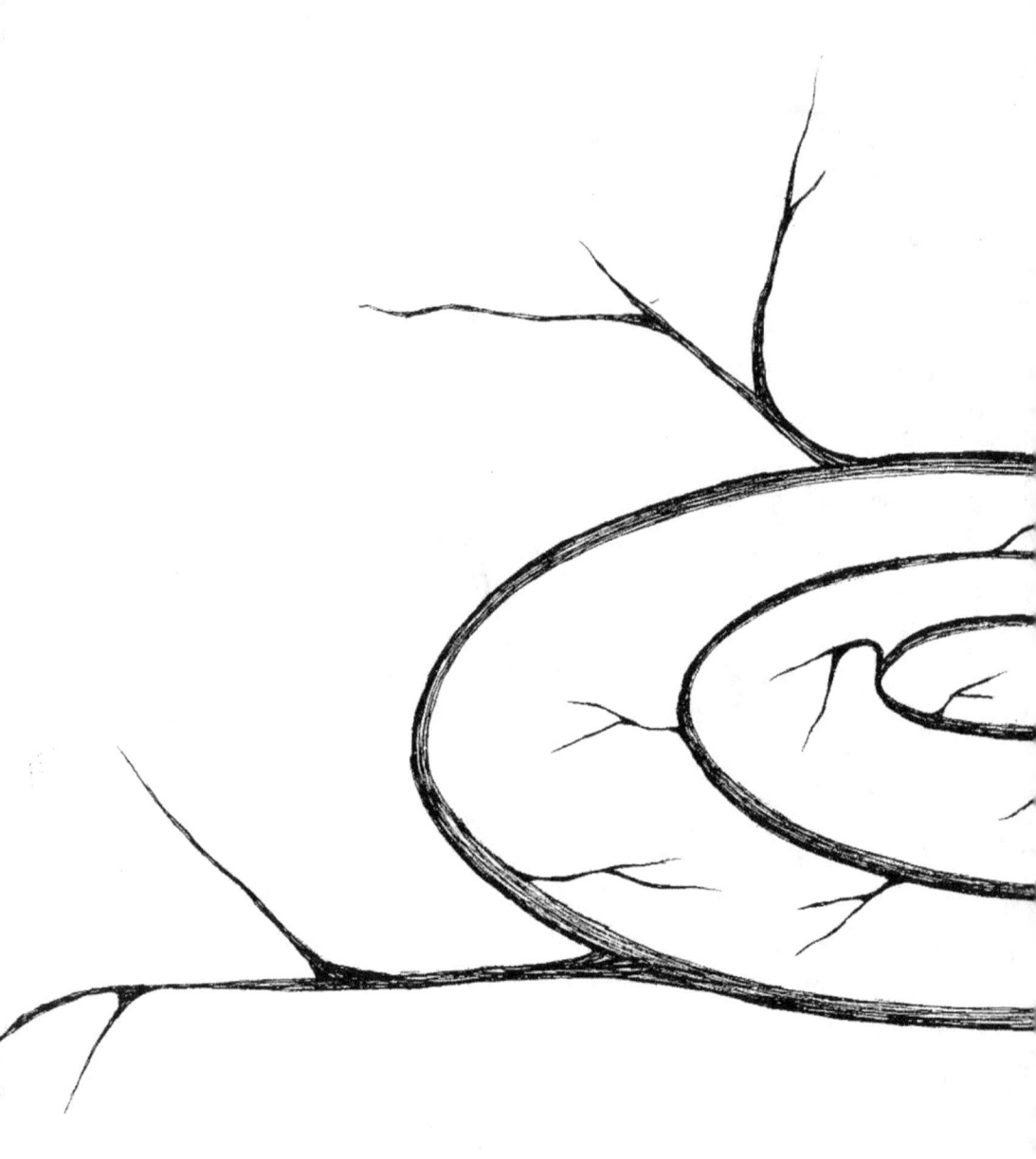

Earth Star
Deep is the anchor
Earth star
I shall not waver

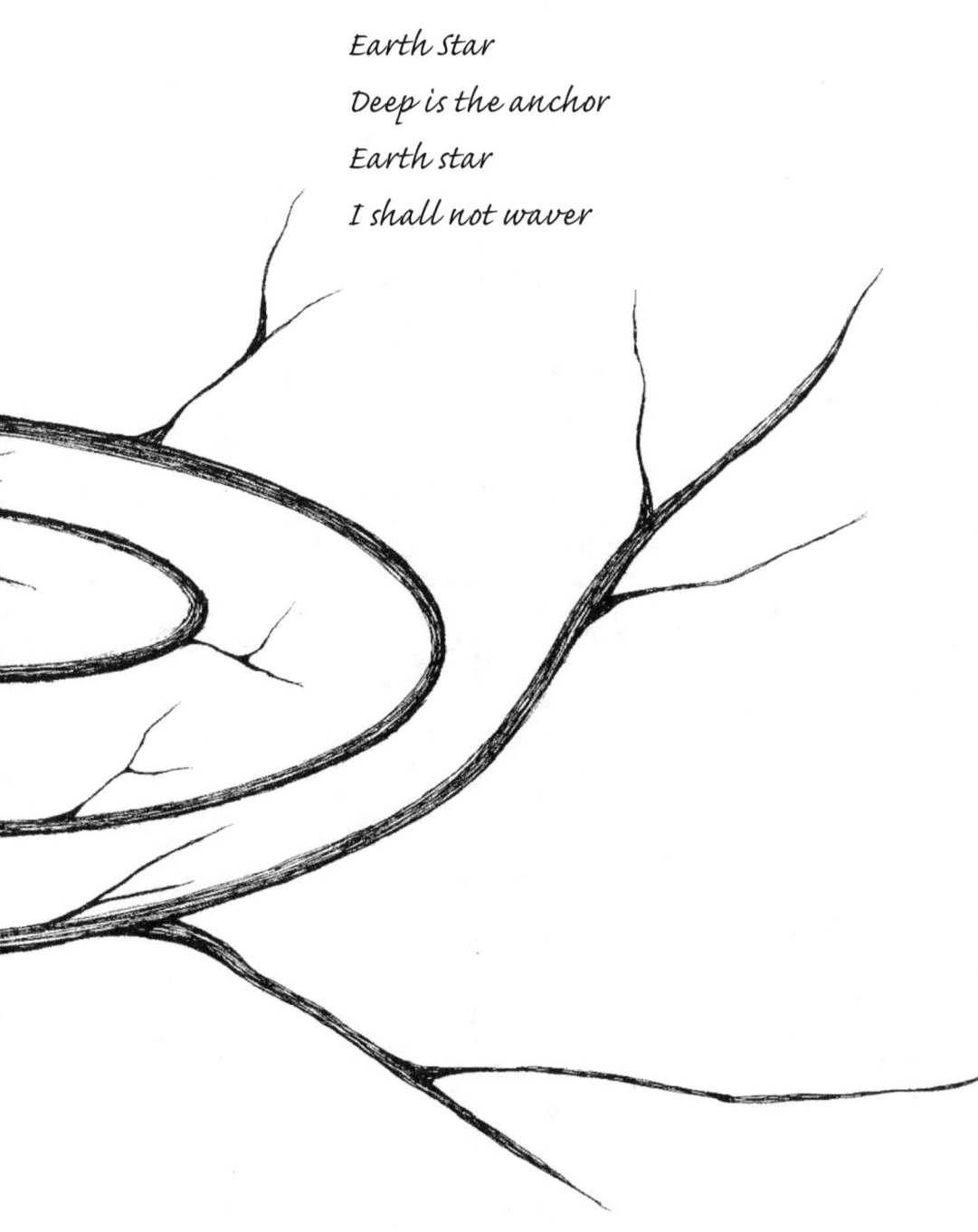

Soul star
I reach up in the sky
Soul star
Clarity in my sight

I am me
You are you
I am you
You are me

In death
Am I born again

Take the leap of faith
Be borne on the angel's wings
Take the leap of faith
Home from my wandering

www.ingramcontent.com/pod-product-compliance
Lightning Source LLC
Chambersburg PA
CBHW052115110526
44592CB00013B/1621